interchange

THIRD EDITION

Jack C. Richards
with Jonathan Hull and Susan Proctor

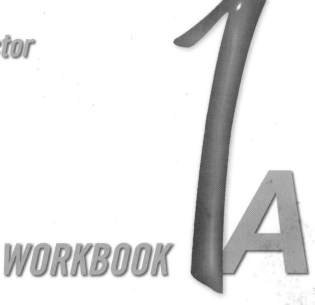

WORKBOOK 1A

CAMBRIDGE UNIVERSITY PRESS
Cambridge, New York, Melbourne, Madrid, Cape Town,
Singapore, São Paulo, Delhi, Mexico City

Cambridge University Press
32 Avenue of the Americas, New York, NY 10013–2473, USA

www.cambridge.org
Information on this title: www.cambridge.org/9780521601788

First published 2005
20th printing 2013

Interchange Third Edition Workbook 1A has been developed from *New Interchange*
Workbook 1A, first published by Cambridge University Press in 1997

Printed in Hong Kong, China, by Golden Cup Printing Company Limited

A catalog record for this publication is available from the British Library.

ISBN 978-0-521-60178-8 Workbook

Art direction, book design, photo research, and layout services: Adventure House, NYC

Contents

Acknowledgments

Illustrations

Rob De Bank 7, 48
Travis Foster 16
Jeff Grunewald 17 (*first and fourth columns*)
Randy Jones 1, 9, 12, 21, 36, 46, 47

Mark Kaufman 13 (*bottom*), 17 (*second, third, and fifth columns*)
Ben Shannon 5, 13 (*top*), 23, 35
Dan Vasconcellos 11, 14, 25
Sam Viviano 2, 3, 15, 42

Photo credits

4 (*clockwise from top left*) © George Ancona/International Stock;
© Superstock; © David R. Frazier/Photo Researchers; © Noblestock/
International Stock
6 © Fotosearch
8 (*clockwise from upper left*) © Zigy Kaluzny/Getty Images;
© Mugshots/Corbis; © Gabe Palmer/Corbis; © Adam Smith/Getty
Images; © John Riley/Getty Images
10 (*from top to bottom*) © Frank Herholdt/Getty Images; Phyllis
Picardi/International Stock; Larry Gatz/Getty Images
18 (*clockwise from left*) © The Sharper Image 1-800-344-4444;
© The Sharper Image 1-800-344-4444; © The Sharper Image
1-800-344-4444; © The Sharp Wizard OZ 5600 electronic organizer
19 (*top to bottom*) © Jennifer Graylock/AP/Wide World Photos;
© Tammy Arroyo/AP/Wide World Photos
20 (*clockwise from top left*) © Neal Preston/Corbis; © Mark Seliger/
Virgin Records; © Scott McKiernan/Getty Images; © Munawar
Hosain/Getty Images; (*bottom*) © Photofest
23 © Warner Brothers Television/Getty Images

24 (*top to bottom*) © Richard Drew/AP/Wide World Photos;
© The Everett Collection
26 (*left to right*) © Donald C. Johnson/Corbis; © Alan Smith/
Getty Images
27 (*top to bottom*) © Simone Huber/Getty Images; © Anthony
Edgeworth/Corbis; © Bill Aron/Photo Researchers; © Dan Bosler/
Getty Images; © Graham Harris/Getty Images
30 (*left to right*) © Bill Losh/Getty Images; © Paul Barton/Corbis
31 (*clockwise from top*) © Dave Rosenberg/Getty Images; © Jim
Cummins/Getty Images; © Alan Becker/Getty Images
33 © age Fotostock
34 (*clockwise from top left*) © Jean Francois Causse/Getty Images;
© Paul Elson/Getty Images; © Dick Dickenson/International Stock
37 © Superstock
38 (*left to right*) © Martin Riedl/Getty Images; © Getty Images
40 © Benjamin Rondel/Corbis
41 (*top to bottom*) © William E. Townsend/Photo Researchers;
© Clem Hager/Photo Researchers

1 Please call me Beth.

1 ***Write about yourself.***

My first name is ___Nejma___ .
My last name is ___Guizani___ .
Please call me ___Najla.___ .
I'm from ___Tunisia.___ .

2 ***Put the words in order to make questions. Then answer the questions.***

1. name   your   what's   last   teacher's
   A: _What's your teacher's last name_ ?
   B: _My teacher's last name is_ .

2. name   your   what's   first   teacher's
   A: _what's your teacher's first name._ ?
   B: _My teacher's first name is Layla._ .

3. from   your   teacher   where   is
   A: _where is your teacher from_ ?
   B: _She's from Tunisia._ .

4. class   your   how   English   is
   A: _How is your English class_ ?
   B: _it's good._ .

5. classmates   what   your   are   like
   A: _what are your classmates like._ ?
   B: _they're freindly._ .

1

Choose the correct responses.

1. A: Hi, I'm Nicole.

   B: _Oh, hi. I'm Michael._

   - Oh, hi. I'm Michael.
   - What do people call you?

2. A: My name is Young Hoon Park.

   B: _Nice to meet you, young Hoon._

   - Nice to meet you, Young Hoon.
   - Let's go and say hello.

3. A: Hello. I'm a new club member.

   B: _Welcome_

   - Thanks.
   - Welcome.

4. A: I'm sorry. What's your name again?

   B: _Joe King_

   - K-I-N-G.
   - Joe King.

5. A: How do you spell your first name?

   B: _A-N-T-O-N-I-O_

   - I'm Antonio.
   - A-N-T-O-N-I-O.

6. A: What do people call you?

   B: _Everyone calls me Ken._

   - It's Ken Tanaka.
   - Everyone calls me Ken.

Look at the answers. What are the questions?

1. Jim: What _'s your first name?_

   Bob: My first name's Bob.

2. Jim: What _'s your last name?_

   Bob: My last name's Hayes.

3. Jim: Who _'s that?_

   Bob: That's my wife.

4. Jim: What _'s her name?_

   Bob: Her name is Rosa.

5. Jim: Where _'s she from?_

   Bob: She's from Mexico.

6. Jim: Who _are they?_

   Bob: They're my wife's parents.

Choose the correct words.

1. They're my classmates. _Their_ names are Noriko and Kate.   (They / Their)
2. We're students. _our_ classroom number is 108-C.   (Our / We)
3. Excuse me. What's _your_ last name again?   (you / your)
4. That's Mr. Kim. _his_ is in my class.   (He / His)
5. _My_ name is Elizabeth. Please call me Liz.   (I / My)
6. This is Paul's wife. _her_ name is Jennifer.   (His / Her)
7. My parents are on vacation. _they_ are in Korea.   (We / They)
8. I'm from Venice, Italy. _It_ is a beautiful city.   (It / It's)

6

Complete this conversation with am, are, or is.

Lisa: Who _are_ the men over there, Amy?

Amy: Oh, they _are_ on the volleyball team. Let me introduce you.

Hi, Surachai, this _is_ Lisa Neil.

Surachai: Pleased to meet you, Lisa.

Lisa: Nice to meet you, too. Where _are_ you from?

Surachai: I _am_ from Thailand.

Amy: And this _is_ Mario. He _is_ from Brazil.

Lisa: Hi, Mario.

A Read these four student biographies. Then complete the chart below.

INTERNATIONAL 🌐 LANGUAGE 🌐 SCHOOL

Every month, we introduce new students to the school. This month, we want to introduce four new students to you. Please say "hello" when you see them in school.

Mario is in English 101. He is from Cali, Colombia. His first language is Spanish, and he also speaks a little French. He wants to be on the school volleyball team. He says he doesn't play very well, but he wants to learn!

Eileen is in Mario's class. She is from Mozambique, in southern Africa. She speaks Swahili and Portuguese. She is studying English and engineering. She wants to be an engineer. She says she does not play any sports, but she wants to make a lot of new friends in her class.

Su Yin is in English 102. She is from Taiwan. She says she can write and read English pretty well, but she needs a lot of practice speaking English. Her first language is Chinese. In her free time, she wants to play volleyball on the school team.

Finally, meet Ahmed. He is in English 103. He says he can speak a lot of English, but his writing is very bad! Ahmed is from Luxor in Egypt, and his first language is Arabic. He is a baseball player, and he wants to be on the school baseball team.

Name	Where from?	Languages	Sports?
1. *Mario*			
2. _____	*Mozambique, Africa*		
3. _____		*Chinese and English*	
4. _____			*baseball*

B Write a short biography of a classmate.

_____

_____

_____

_____

8

Choose the correct sentences to complete this conversation.

> ☐ And what are you studying?
> ☐ No, she's not. She's my sister!
> ☑ Hi, Sarah. I'm Rich. How are you?
> ☐ Oh, really? Is Susan Miller in your class?
> ☐ No, I'm not. I'm on vacation. Are you a student?

Sarah: Hello, I'm Sarah.

Rich: *Hi, Sarah. I'm Rich. How are you?*

Sarah: Pretty good, thanks. Are you a student here?

Rich: No, I'm not. I'm on vacation. Are you a student?

Sarah: Yes, I am.

Rich: And what are you studying?

Sarah: I'm studying Spanish.

Rich: Oh, really. Is Susan Miller in your class?

Sarah: Yes, she is. Is she your friend?

Rich: No, she's not. She is my sister?

9

Complete this conversation. Use contractions where possible.

Grammar note: Contractions

Do not use contractions for short answers with Yes.

Are you from Argentina?   Is he from Greece?

   Yes, I am. (*not* Yes, I'm.)   Yes, he is. (*not* Yes, he's.)

Alex: Hello. _____ I'm _____ Alex Lam.

And this is my sister Amy.

Tina: Hi. _____ I'm. _____ Tina Fernandez.

Amy: Are you from South America, Tina?

Tina: Yes, I am . I'm from Argentina.

Where are you and your sister from, Alex?

Alex: We are from Taiwan.

Tina: Are you from Taipei?

Alex: No, we are not . we are from Tainan.

Say, are you in English 101?

Tina: No, I'm not . I'm in English 102.

10 Look at the answers. What are the questions?

1. A: _Are you on vacation here?_

   B: No, I'm not on vacation. I'm a student here.

2. A: _Are you free?_

   B: No, I'm not. I'm very busy.

3. A: _Are you from Spain_

   B: No, we're not from Spain. We're from Mexico.

4. A: _is your teacher Mr Brown? / is Mr Brown your teacher?_

   B: No, my teacher isn't Mr. Brown. I'm in Ms. West's class.

5. A: _Are Kim and Mika in your class?_

   B: Yes, Kim and Mika are in my class.

6. A: _is it an interesting class? / is your class interesting?_

   B: Yes, it's an interesting class.

7. A: _Are they on the same baseball team?_

   B: No, they're not on the same baseball team. They're on

   the same volleyball team.

11 Look at the expressions. Which ones say "hello" and which ones say "good-bye"?

	Hello	Good-bye
1. How are you doing?	✓	☐
2. See you around.	☐	✓
3. So long.	☐	✓
4. How's everything?	✓	☐
5. Long time, no see.	✓	☐
6. See you Monday.	☐	✓
7. Have a good weekend.	☐	✓
8. Hi there!	✓	☐

12 Answer these questions about yourself. Use contractions where possible.

1. Are you from South America? _No, I'm not. I'm from Tunisia_

2. Are you on vacation? _No, I'm not. I'm in Ameasit_

3. Are you a student at a university? _No, I'm not. I'm a student in Ameadist_

4. Is your English class in the morning? _No. It's not. It's in the evening._

5. Is your teacher from England? _No, she's not. she is from slotland_

6. Is your first name "popular"? _No, It's not. It's umpopular._

2 How do you spend your day?

1 *Match the words in columns A and B. Write the names of the jobs.*

A	B	
☑ company	☑ designer	1. *company director*
☑ computer	☑ director	2. *computer programmer*
☑ disc	☑ guard	3. *disc jockey*
☑ fashion	☑ guide	4. *fashion designer*
☑ security	☐ jockey	5. *security guard*
☑ tour	☑ programmer	6. *tour guide*

2 *Write sentences using He or She.*

1. I'm a computer programmer. I work in an office. I like computers a lot.

   He's a computer programmer.
   He works in an office
   He likes computers a lot

2. I work in a nightclub. I'm a disc jockey. I play music.

   She works in a nightclub. She's a disc jockey
   she plays music.

3. I'm a security guard. I work in a department store. I guard the store at night.

   He's a security guard. He works in a
   department store. He guards the store at
   night

4. I work in a design studio. I create beautiful fashions. I'm a fashion designer.

   She's a fashion designer
   she creates beautiful fashions
   she's a fashion designer

7

3 Write a or an in the correct places.

> ### Grammar note: Articles a and an
>
> Use **a** + singular noun before a consonant sound.
> Use **an** + singular noun before a vowel sound.
>
> He is **a c**arpenter.   He is **an a**rchitect.
> He is **a g**ood carpenter.   He is **an e**xpensive architect.
>
> *Do not use* **a** *or* **an** + *plural nouns.*
> They are good carpenter**s**.   They are expensive architect**s**.

1. He's *a* carpenter. He works for *a* construction
   company. He builds schools and hospitals.

2. She works for travel company and
   arranges tours. She's *a* travel agent.

3. He has difficult job. He's *a* cashier.
   He works in supermarket.

4. She's *an* architect. She works for large company.
   She builds houses. It's interesting job.

5. She works with computers in *a* office.
   She's Web-site designer. She's *an* also part-time
   student. She takes English class in
   the evening.

4 Choose someone in your family. Write about his or her job.

_____

_____

_____

_____

5 **Complete this conversation with the correct words.**

Tom: What ___does___ your husband ___do___ exactly?
　　　　　(do / does)　　　　　　　　(do / does)

Liz: He _works_ for a department store. He's a store manager.
　　　(work / works)

Tom: How _does_ he _like_ it?
　　　　(do / does)　(like / likes)

Liz: It's an interesting job. He _likes_ it very much.
　　　　　　　　　　　　　　(like / likes)

　　But he _works_ long hours. And what ___do___ you ___do___ ?
　　　　(work / works)　　　　　　　(do / does)　　(do / does)

Tom: I'm a student. I _study_ architecture.
　　　　　　　　(study / studies)

Liz: Oh, really? Where ___do___ you ___go___ to school?
　　　　　　　　(do / does)　　(go / goes)

Tom: I ___go___ to Lincoln University. My girlfriend ___goes___ there, too.
　　　(go / goes)　　　　　　　　　　　　(go / goes)

Liz: Really? And what ___does___ she ___study___ ?
　　　　　　　　(do / does)　(study / studies)

Tom: She _studies_ hotel management.
　　　　(study / studies)

Liz: That sounds interesting.

6 **Complete the questions in this conversation.**

Mark: Where _do you work?_

Victor: I work for American Express.

Mark: And what _do you do_ there?

Victor: I'm in management.

Mark: How _do you like it?/How is it/what is it like_

Victor: It's a great job. And what _do you do?_

Mark: I'm a salesperson.

Victor: Really? What _do you do exactly?/_
　　　　　　　　　　　=sell

Mark: I sell computers. Do you want to buy one?

7 **Read these two interviews, and answer the questions.**

Today, *Job Talk* interviews two people with interesting jobs.

Job Talk: Felix, where do you work?

Felix: I work at home, and I work in Southeast Asia.

Job Talk: Really? Well, what do you do at home?

Felix: I'm a chef. I practice cooking new things, and then I write cookbooks.

Job Talk: That sounds interesting. And what do you do in Southeast Asia?

Felix: I make TV programs about Thai cooking.

Job Talk: You have an interesting life, Felix.

Felix: Yes, but it's hard work!

Job Talk: How do you like your job, Julia?

Julia: I love it, but I work long hours.

Job Talk: Do you work late?

Julia: Yes, I work until eight or nine o'clock in the evening. But I take three or four hours for lunch.

Job Talk: Really! But what do you do exactly?

Julia: I stay in all the best new hotels and . . .

Job Talk: Are you a hotel manager?

Julia: No, I'm an electrician! I do the electrical work in new hotels.

1. What does Felix do? _He_ _____
2. What does he do at home? _____
3. What does he do in Southeast Asia? _____
4. What does Julia do? _She_ _____
5. When does she finish work? _____
6. How does she like her job? _____

8 **Meet Pat. Write questions about him using What, Where, When, and How.**

1. _What does he do?_
2. _where does he work?_
3. _when does he work?_
4. _How does he like?_

MERCY HOSPITAL

Patrick Kennedy

Registered Nurse/Night Shift

9 How does Pat spend his weekends? Complete this paragraph with the words from the list.

☑ around ☑ at ☑ before ☑ early ☑ in ☑ late ☑ on ☑ until

Everyone knows Pat at the hospital. Pat is a part-time nurse. He works at night on weekends. ___On___ Saturdays and Sundays, Pat sleeps most of the day and wakes up a little _before_ nine _in_ the evening, usually at 8:45 or 8:50. He has breakfast very late, _around_ 9:30 or 10:00 P.M.! He watches television _until_ eleven o'clock, and then starts work _at_ midnight. _early_ in the morning, usually around 5:00 A.M., he leaves work, has a little snack, goes home, goes to bed, and sleeps _late_ . It's a perfect schedule for Pat. He's a pre-med student on weekdays at a local college.

10 Use these words to complete the crossword puzzle.

☑ answers ☑ sells ☑ types
☐ does ☐ serves ☑ works
☑ gets ☑ starts ☑ writes
☑ goes ☑ takes

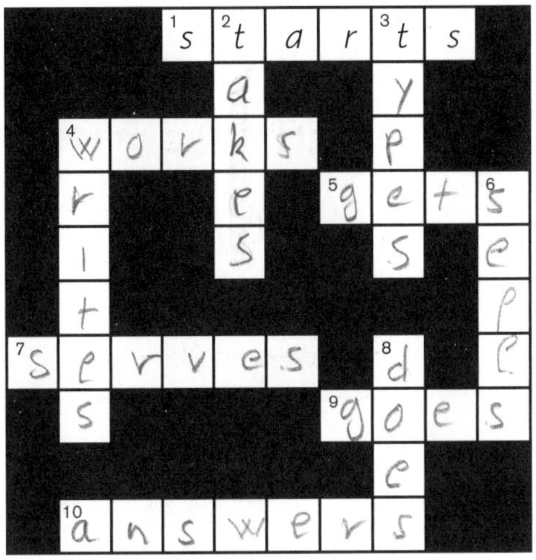

Across

1 Lauren _____ work at 5:00 P.M.

4 Karen _____ in a hospital.

5 Ellen _____ up early in the morning.

7 Seoul Garden _____ good Korean food.

9 Rodney _____ to bed after midnight.

10 Andrea is a receptionist. She _____ the phone and greets people.

Down

2 Linda is a tour guide. She _____ people on tours.

3 Dan _____ 100 words a minute on his new computer.

4 Mei-li _____ about 30 e-mails a week.

6 My father works in a bookstore. He _____ books and magazines.

8 What _____ your sister do?

Crossword grid (handwritten answers):
- 1 Across: starts
- 4 Across: works
- 5 Across: gets
- 7 Across: serves
- 9 Across: goes
- 10 Across: answers
- 2 Down: takes
- 3 Down: types
- 4 Down: writes
- 6 Down: sells
- 8 Down: does

11 Choose the sentences in the box that have the same meaning as the sentences below.

- ☐ He goes to the university.
- ☐ She serves food in a restaurant.
- ☐ She stays up late.
- ☐ What does he do?
- ☑ He's an aerobics teacher.
- ☐ He works part time.

1. He teaches aerobics.
   He's an aerobics teacher.

2. Where does he work?
   what does he do

3. She's a waitress.
   she serves food in a restaurant.

4. He's a student.
   He goes to the university

5. She goes to bed at midnight.
   She stays up late

6. He works four hours every day.
   He wroks part time.

12 Fill in the missing words or phrases from these job advertisements.

1. ☐ at night
   ☐ part time
   ☐ weekends
   ☑ nurses

2. ☐ Interesting
   ☐ Spanish
   ☐ tours
   ☐ student

3. ☐ manager
   ☐ long hours
   ☐ restaurant
   ☐ until

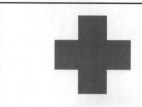

New York Hospital needs

_____nurses_____.

Work during the day or
at night, weekdays or
weekends, full time
or _part time_.

Call 614-555-1191.

interesting
job for a language
student.
Mornings only. Take people on
tours. Need good
English and _spanish_.

Call 917-555-3239.

No need to work
long hours !
Only work from 6:00
until 11:00
four evenings a week.
Our _manager_
serves great food! Work
as our _restaurant_

Call 308-555-6845.

How much is it?

1 **Choose the correct sentences to complete this conversation.**

- ☐ Which one?
- ☑ Which ones?
- ☐ Oh, Sam. Thank you very much.
- ☐ Well, I like it, but it's expensive.
- ☐ Yes. But I don't really like light blue.

Sam: Look at those pants, Rebecca.

Rebecca: _Which ones?_

Sam: The light blue ones over there. They're nice.

Rebecca: _yes. But I don't really like light blue._

Sam: Hmm. Well, what about that sweater? It's perfect for you.

Rebecca: _which one._

Sam: This red one.

Rebecca: _well. I like it, but it's expensive_

Sam: Hey, let me buy it for you. It's a present!

Rebecca: _oh. Sam. thank you very much._

2 **Complete these conversations with How much is / are . . . ?**
and this, that, these, or those.

1. A: _How much is this_ _____ backpack?

   B: It's $31.99.

2. A: _How much are those._ bracelets?

   B: They're $29.

3. A: _How much are these._ shoes?

   B: They're $64.

4. A: _How much is this_ dog?

   B: That's *my* dog, and he's not for sale!

3 **Write the plurals of these words.**

1. backpack _backpacks_
2. company _companies_
3. dress _dresses_
4. day _days_
5. glove _gloves_
6. hairbrush _hair brushes_

7. necklace _necklaces_
8. ring _ringes_
9. scarf _scarfes_
10. sweater _swreateres_
11. tie _ties_
12. box _boxes_

4 **What do you think of these prices? Write a response.**

> That's cheap.   That's not bad.   That's reasonable.   That's pretty expensive!

1. $90 for a polyester tie
   That's pretty expensive!

2. $150 for gold earrings
   that's reasonable

3. $500 for a silk dress
   that's pretty expensive

4. $40 for leather gloves
   that's cheap.

5. $2,000 for a computer
   that's reasonable

6. $5 for two plastic hairbrushes
   that's reasonable.

7. $15 for a silver necklace
   that's not bad.

5   *Choose the correct words to complete the conversations.*

1. Clerk: Good afternoon.

   Luis: Oh, hi. How much is ____*this*____ watch?
   (this / these)

   Clerk: __It's__ $195.
   (It's / They're)

   Luis: And how much is that ____one____ ?
   (one / ones)

   Clerk: __It's__ $255.
   (It's / They're)

   Luis: Oh, really? Well, thanks, anyway.

2. Kim: Excuse me. How much are ____those____ jeans?
   (that / those)

   Clerk: __they're__ only $59.
   (It's / They're)

   Kim: And how much is ____this____ sweater?
   (this / these)

   Clerk: Which __one__ ? They're all different.
   (one / ones)

   Kim: I like this green ____one____ .
   (one / ones)

   Clerk: __It's__ $34.
   (It's / They're)

   Kim: Well, that's not bad.

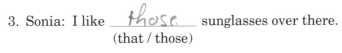

3. Sonia: I like ____those____ sunglasses over there.
   (that / those)

   Clerk: Which ____ones____ ?
   (one / ones)

   Sonia: The small brown ____ones____ .
   (one / ones)

   Clerk: __they're__ $199.
   (It's / They're)

   Sonia: Oh, they're expensive!

6 *What do you make out of these materials? Complete the chart using words from the list. (You will use words more than once.)*

| boots | pants | bracelet | ring | gloves | shirt | jacket | necklace |

Cotton	Gold	Leather	Silk	Plastic	Wool
pants	necklace bracelet	jacket gloves	shirt	bracelet	gloves jacket

7 *Make comparisons using the words given. Add* than *if necessary.*

cotton gloves

leather gloves

1. A: These cotton gloves are nice.
   B: Yes, but the leather ones are _____nicer_____ . (nice)
   A: They're also ___more___ . (expensive)

2. A: Those silk jackets look
      ___more attractive than___
      the wool ones. (attractive)
   B: Yes, but the wool ones are
      ___warmer___ . (warm)

silk jackets

wool jackets

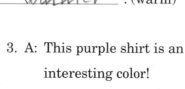

purple shirt

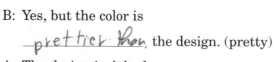

red shirt

3. A: This purple shirt is an interesting color!
   B: Yes, but the color is
      ___prettier than___ the design. (pretty)
   A: The design isn't bad.
   B: I think the pattern on that red shirt
      is ___better than___ the pattern on
      this purple one. (good)

4. A: Hey, look at this gold ring! It's nice.
      And it's ___cheaper than___ that silver ring. (cheap)
   B: But it's ___smaller than___ the silver one. (small)

gold ring

silver ring

   A: Well, yeah. The silver one is ___bigger than___ the gold one. (big)
      But look at the price tag. One thousand dollars is a lot of money!

8 Complete the chart. Use the words from the list.

- ☑ athletic shoes
- ☑ bracelet
- ☑ cap
- ☑ CD player
- ☑ dress
- ☑ earrings
- ☑ laptop computer
- ☑ necklace
- ☑ ring
- ☐ sweater
- ☐ television
- ☐ video camera

Clothing	Electronics	Jewelry
athletic shoes	cD player	bracePet
cap	laptop computer	earrings
dress	television	necklace
s\veater	video camera	ring

9 Answer these questions. Give your own information.

1 black sunglasses   **2** wool cap   **3** high-top shoes   **4** laptop computer   **5** 19-inch television

white sunglasses   leather cap   tennis shoes   desktop computer   25-inch television

1. Which ones do you prefer, the black sunglasses or the white sunglasses?
   I prefer the black ones.

2. Which cap do you like more, the wool one or the leather one?
   I like the wool one more

3. Which ones do you like more, the high-tops or the tennis shoes?
   I like the tennis shots ones   because they're more attractin

4. Which one do you prefer, the laptop computer or the desktop computer?
   I prefer the laptop one because it convenie¬t

5. Which television do you like better, the 19-inch one or the 25-inch one?
   I like the 19-inch more why: because is eary

10 *Great electronic gadgets!*

1 ___

2 ___

3 ___

4 ___

A Match the ads and the pictures.

a. Find the correct spelling and pronunciation of more than 80,000 words with this electronic dictionary! Made of strong plastic. Comes in two colors – dark gray or light blue. $104.50.

b. Problems with a crossword puzzle? Try this crossword puzzle solver! Simply key in the letters you know and a "?" for the ones you don't know. In seconds, the gadget fills the blanks. Has a database of 130,000 words. Great value at only $49.95.

c. Watch your favorite baseball game at work or at school! This TV fits in your pocket, only 6" × 1" (15 cm × 2 cm). Gives an excellent picture. Yours for only $299.50.

d. Use the electronic address book for the names and addresses of all your friends. Takes up to 400 names, addresses, and phone numbers. Plastic case included. Regular model $59.95. Desktop model available for $64.95.

B Check (✓) True or False.

	True	False
1. The electronic dictionary comes in many colors.	☐	☐
2. The crossword puzzle solver can find the answers.	☐	☐
3. The pocket television is about $300.	☐	☐
4. The desktop model of the electronic address book is more expensive than the regular model.	☐	☐

C What's special about an electronic gadget or another item you have? Write a paragraph about it.

_____

_____

_____

_____

_____

_____

4 Do you like rap?

1 Check (✓) the boxes to complete the survey about music and movies.

1 How often do you listen to these types of music?

	Often	Sometimes	Not often
pop			✓
classical		✓	
gospel	✓		
rock		✓	
jazz	✓		

2 How often do you watch these types of movies?

	Often	Sometimes	Not often
science fiction	✓		
horror films			✓
thrillers		✓	
westerns	✓		
comedies		✓	

2 What do you think of these kinds of entertainment? Answer the questions with the expressions and pronouns in the box.

Yes, I do.
I love . . .
I like . . . a lot.

No, I don't.
I don't like . . . very much.
I can't stand . . .

Object pronouns
him
her
it
them

Justin Timberlake

Beyoncé Knowles

1. Do you like salsa?
   Yes, I do. I like it a lot.

2. Do you like Justin Timberlake?
   Yes, I do, I like him a lot.

3. Do you like rap?
   I don't like it very much.

4. Do you like Beyoncé Knowles?
   yes I do, I like her a lot

5. Do you like reality TV shows?
   yes I do. I like them a lot

6. Do you like soap operas?
   I don't like them very much

3 Choose the correct job for each picture.

☐ an actor   ☐ a rock band   ☐ a singer   ☐ a TV talk show host

1. Julio Iglesias is *an actor*

2. The Rolling Stones are *a rock band*

3. Oprah Winfrey is *a TV talk show host*

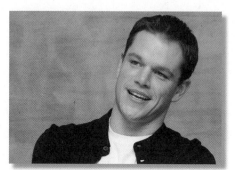

4. Matt Damon is *a singer*

4 Complete these conversations.

1. Ed: ___*Do*___ you ___*like*___ country music, Sarah?

   Sarah: Yes, I *like* it a lot. I'm a real fan of Garth Brooks.

   Ed: Oh, *does* he play the guitar?

   Sarah: Yes, he *does*. He's my favorite musician.

2. Anne: *what* kind of music *do*

   your parents *like*, Jason?

   Jason: They *like* classical music.

   Anne: Who *do* they *like*? Mozart?

   Jason: No, they *don't* like him very much. They prefer Beethoven.

3. Scott: Teresa, *do* you *like* Christina Aguilera?

   Teresa: No, I *don't*. I can't stand her. I like Pink.

   Scott: I don't know her. What kind of music *does* she sing?

   Teresa: She *sings* pop songs. She's really great!

Garth Brooks

5 **Complete these questions and write answers.**

1. _What kinds_ of movies do you like?   _I like_ _____

2. ___what.___ is your favorite movie?   _My favorite_ _____

3. _what kinds_ of TV shows do you like?   _____

4. ___what___ is your favorite TV actor or actress? _____

5. ___what.___ is your favorite song?   _____

6. ___what___ is your favorite rock band?   _____

6 **What do you think? Answer the questions.**

funny

scary

1. Which films are funnier, horror films or comedies?
   Comedies are funnier than horror films.

2. Which movies are more interesting, musicals or science fiction films?
   science fiction films are more interesting than musicals.

3. Which films are scarier, horror films or thrillers?
   horrorfilms are scarier than thrillers

4. Which films are more exciting, westerns or crime thrillers?
   crime thrillers are more exciting than westerns.

7 Verbs and nouns

A Which nouns often go with these verbs? Complete the chart. Use each noun only once.

listen to	play	watch
jazz	the piano	videos
music	the guitar	the news
the trumpet	CDs	a film

- ☐ the piano
- ☐ videos
- ☑ jazz
- ☐ the news
- ☐ music
- ☐ the guitar
- ☐ a film
- ☐ the trumpet
- ☐ CDs

B Write a sentence using each verb in part A.

1. _____

2. _____

3. _____

8 Movie reviews

A Read these movie reviews. Choose a title from the box for each review.

House of Laughs   The Best Man Wins   Ahead of Time   Coming Up for Air

1. _____

What are high school kids like in the future? Do you ever wonder? If so, see this movie! The story is about a group of normal 21st century high school kids. After class one day they find a time machine behind the school. One of the teens sees a button marked "2500" and clicks on it. They immediately travel to the beginning of the 26th century. Do they get back in time for school the next day? Watch and find out. ★★★★

2. _____

There are lots and lots of laughs in this movie. It's about a group of young people in London. They all live in the same house in a suburb far from the city center. The characters come from different countries. They speak different languages, so they often have misunderstandings. The script is very funny and the acting is very good. This movie is like a really good TV soap opera. You'll love it! ★★★★★

3. _____

The action never stops in this movie. Police officer Karen Montana wants to catch Mr. X, a mysterious gold thief. Mr. X is stealing gold from an underwater shipwreck. Before Ms. Montana can catch him, she has to learn how to use diving equipment. But every time she goes underwater, he swims to the surface. Of course, she finally catches him, but not until the final minute of this very long film. ★★

B What kind of movie is each one in part A?

1. ☐ a horror film
   ☐ a science fiction film
   ☐ a historical drama

2. ☐ a travel film
   ☐ a western
   ☐ a comedy

3. ☐ a romantic comedy
   ☐ a crime thriller
   ☐ a documentary

9 Choose the correct responses.

1. A: What do you think of *Friends*?

   B: <u>I'm not a real fan of the show.</u>

   - How about you?
   - I'm not a real fan of the show.

2. A: Do you like gospel music?

   B: <u>I can't stand it.</u>

   - I can't stand it.
   - I can't stand them.

3. A: There's a baseball game tonight.

   B: <u>Great. Let's go.</u>

   - Thanks. I'd love to.
   - Great. Let's go.

4. A: Would you like to see a movie this weekend?

   B: <u>that sounds great.</u>

   - That sounds great!
   - I don't agree.

the cast of *Friends*

10 Yes or no?

A Young Ha is inviting friends to a movie. Do they accept the invitation or not? Check (✓) Yes or No for each response.

Accept?	Yes	No
1. I'd love to. What time does it start?	✓	☐
2. Thanks, but I'm not a real fan of his.	☐	☐
3. That sounds great. Where is it?	☐	☐
4. I'd love to, but I have to work until midnight.	☐	☐
5. Thanks. I'd really like to. When do you want to meet?	☐	☐

B Respond to the invitations.

1. I have tickets to a rap concert on Saturday. Would you like to go?

   _____

2. There's a soccer game tonight. Do you want to go with me?

   _____

3. Britney Spears is performing tomorrow at the stadium. Would you like to see her?

   _____

11 *Choose the correct phrases to complete these conversations.*

1. Robin: _Do you like_ country music, Kate?
   (Do you like / Would you like)

   Kate: Yes, I do. _I like._ it a lot.
   (I like / I'd like)

   Robin: There's a Dixie Chicks concert on Friday.
   would you like. to go with me?
   (Do you like / Would you like)

   Kate: Yes, _I'd love to._ . Thanks.
   (I love to / I'd love to)

2. Carlos: There's a French film tonight at 11:00.
   would you like. to go?
   (Do you like / Would you like)

   Phil: _I'd like to._ , but I have to study tonight.
   (I like to / I'd like to)

   Carlos: Well, _do you like_ Brazilian films?
   (do you like / would you like)

   Phil: Yes, _I do_ . I love them!
   (I do / I would)

   Carlos: There's a great Brazilian movie on TV tomorrow.
   would you like. to watch it with me?
   (Do you like / Would you like)

   Phil: _I'd love to._ . Thanks.
   (I like to / I'd love to)

12 *Rewrite these sentences. Find another way to say each sentence using the words given.*

1. Do you like jazz?

   What do you think of jazz? (think of)

2. Richard doesn't like classical music.

   _____ (can't stand)

3. I think horror films are great!

   _____ (love)

4. Celia doesn't like country music.

   _____ (be a fan of)

5. Do you want to go to a baseball game?

   _____ (would like)

5 Tell me about your family.

1 **Which words are for males? Which are for females? Complete the chart.**

☑ aunt ☑ brother ☐ daughter ☐ father ☐ husband ☐ mother
☐ nephew ☐ niece ☐ sister ☐ son ☐ uncle ☐ wife

Males	Females
brother *father* *husband* *niece* *son* *uncle*	*aunt* *daughter* *wife* *sister* *mother* *nephew*

2 **Complete this conversation. Use the present continuous of the verbs given.**

Joel: You look tired, Don. _Are you studying_ (study)
late at night these days?

Don: No, I'm not. My brother and sister _are staying_ (stay)
with me right now. We go to bed after midnight every night.

Joel: Really? What _are they doing_ (do) this
summer? _are they taking_ (take) classes, too?

Don: No, they aren't. My brother is on vacation now, but he
is looking (look) for a part-time job here.

Joel: What about your sister? _is she working_ (work)?

Don: Yes, she is. She has a part-time job at the university.
What about you, Joel? Are you in school this summer?

Joel: Yes, I am. I _'m studying_ (study) two languages.

Don: Oh, _are you taking_ (take) French and
Spanish again?

Joel: Well, I'm taking Spanish again, but I
'm starting (start) Japanese.

Don: Really? That's exciting!

Rewrite these sentences. Find another way to say each sentence using the words given.

1. Joseph is Maria's uncle.
   Maria is Joseph's niece. _____ (niece)

2. Liz is married to Peter.
   Peter is _____ (husband)

3. Isabel is Frank's and Liza's granddaughter.
   _____ (grandparents)

4. We have two children.
   _____ (son and daughter)

5. My wife's father is a painter.
   _____ (father-in-law)

6. Michael does not have a job right now.
   _____ (look for)

Choose the correct sentences to complete this conversation.

San Francisco

Honolulu

- ☐ Yes, he is. He loves it there.
- ☑ No, I'm not. I'm living in Honolulu now.
- ☐ Yes, we are. We really love San Francisco.
- ☐ Yes, I do. I like it a lot.
- ☐ No, they aren't. They're living in New York these days.

Chris: Are you still living in San Francisco, Philip?

Philip: *No, I'm not. I'm living in Honolulu now.* _____

Chris: Wow! Do you like it?

Philip: _____

Chris: And is your brother still working in Hong Kong?

Philip: _____

Chris: And how about your parents? Are they still living in Florida?

Philip: _____

How about you and your family, Chris? Are you still living here?

Chris: _____

5 **Complete these sentences. Use the simple present or the present continuous of the verbs given.**

1. This is my aunt Barbara.

   She lives _____ (live) in Rome, but

   _____ (visit) Chile this summer.

   _____ (have) a second home there.

2. And these are my parents.

   _____ (work) in London,

   but _____ (visit) my aunt in Chile

   this month.

3. And here you can see my grandparents.

   _____ (live) in New York, but

   _____ (stay) at my parents' house

   in London now.

4. This is my brother-in-law Edward.

   _____ (want) to be a company

   director. _____ (study) business

   in Canada right now.

5. And this is my niece Christina.

   _____ (go) to high school.

   _____ (like) mathematics, but

   she doesn't like English.

6 **Choose a friend or family member. Write about him or her using the simple present and present continuous.**

_____

_____

_____

_____

A   Answer these questions. Then read the passage.

1. At what age do most young people leave their parents' home in your country? _____

2. Do some young people live with their parents after they get married? _____

Leaving Home

Young people leave their parents' homes at different ages in different parts of the world.

In the United States, a lot of college students do not live at home. They often choose to go to college in different cities – away from their parents. At college, many live in university housing. After college, most people prefer to live in their own homes. They often live alone, but some people rent apartments with others.

These people are called *roommates*. By the age of 22, few young people in the United States live with their parents.

Families stay together longer in many Asian countries and cities. In Hong Kong, for example, nearly all university students live with their parents. Rents in the city are very expensive, and few students have the money to pay for their own apartments. Very few young people live alone or become roommates in a shared apartment. Many young people in Hong Kong continue to live with their parents even after they marry.

B   Check (✓) True or False. For statements that are false, write the correct information.

In the United States	True	False
1. Very few students live in university housing. _____	☐	☐
2. Some young adults share apartments with roommates. _____	☐	☐
3. Nearly all young adults live with their parents. _____	☐	☐

In Hong Kong	True	False
4. Not many university students live with their parents. _____	☐	☐
5. Few young people live alone. _____	☐	☐
6. Most young married couples have enough money to live in their own apartments. _____	☐	☐

8 *Arrange the quantifiers from the most to the least.*

☐ a lot of ☑ no   1. *all*   6. _____

☐ most   ☐ few   2. _____   7. _____

☐ a few   ☐ not many 3. _____   8. _____

☐ nearly all ☐ many   4. _____   9. _____

☑ all   ☐ some   5. _____   10. *no*

9 *Rewrite these sentences about the United States using the quantifiers given.*

1. Sixty-five percent of children start school before the age of five. A hundred percent of children go to school after the age of five.

   ☐ all   ☑ many

   Many children start school before the age of five.
   _____

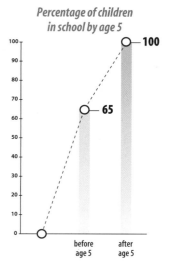

Percentage of children in school by age 5

2. Ninety-five percent of young people get a job after they finish high school. Only 20 percent go to college.

   ☐ nearly all   ☐ a few

   _____

   _____

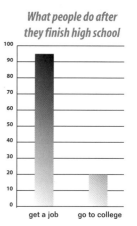

What people do after they finish high school

3. About 30 percent of people over 65 have part-time jobs. Only about 15 percent like to travel abroad. Fifty-five percent like to stay with their grandchildren.

   ☐ many   ☐ not many   ☐ few

   _____

   _____

   _____

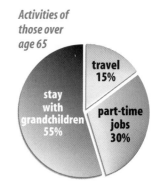

Activities of those over age 65

10 *Choose the correct words or phrases to complete this paragraph.*

In my country, some _____*couples*_____ (couples / cousins / relatives) get married fairly young. Not many marriages _____ (break up / get divorced / stay together), and nearly all _____ (divorced / married / single) people remarry. Elderly couples often _____ (divorce again / move away / live at home) and take care of their grandchildren.

11 *Complete these sentences about your country. Use the words in the box.*

all	nearly all	most	a lot of	some	few	no

1. _____ young people go to the university.
2. _____ people study English.
3. _____ married couples have more than five children.
4. _____ elderly people have part-time jobs.
5. _____ students have full-time jobs.
6. _____ children go to school on Saturdays.

6 How often do you exercise?

1 Complete the chart. Use words from the list.
(Some of the words can be both individual sports and exercise.)

basketball	baseball	aerobics
yoga	jogging	bicycling
swimming	football	tennis
stretching	soccer	volleyball

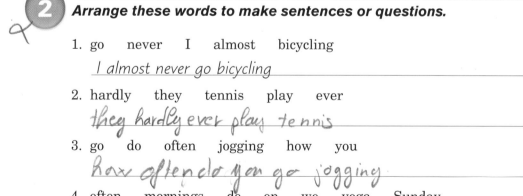

team sport

individual sport

exercise

Team sports	Individual sports	Exercise
basketball		

2 Arrange these words to make sentences or questions.

1. go never I almost bicycling
   <u>I almost never go bicycling</u> .

2. hardly they tennis play ever
   <u>they hardly ever play tennis</u> .

3. go do often jogging how you
   <u>how often do you go jogging</u> ?

4. often mornings do on we yoga Sunday
   <u>we often do yoga on sunday mornings</u> .

5. ever Charlie do does aerobics
   <u>Does charlie ever do aerobics</u> ?

6. do on you what usually Saturdays do
   <u>what do you usually do on saturdays</u> ?

31

3 **Use these questions to complete the conversations.**
How often do you . . . ? Do you ever . . . ? What do you usually . . . ?

1. A: _Do you ever exercise?_

   B: Yes, I often exercise on weekends.

2. A: what do you usually do on Saturdays and Sundays?

   B: Well, I usually do karate on Saturdays and yoga on Sundays.

3. A: Do you ever go to the gym after work?

   B: No, I never go to the gym after work.

4. A: How often do you exercise?

   B: I don't exercise very often at all.

5. A: Do you ever play sports on weekends,

   B: Yes, I sometimes play sports on weekends – usually baseball.

6. A: what do you usually do in your free time?

   B: I usually play tennis in my free time.

4 **Keeping fit?**

A Check (✓) how often you do each of the things in the chart.

	Every day	Once or twice a week	Sometimes	Not very often	Never
do aerobics	☐	☐	☐	☐	☐
do karate	☐	☐	☐	☐	☐
do weight training	☐	☐	☐	☐	☐
go jogging	☐	☐	☐	☐	☐
go swimming	☐	☐	☐	☐	☐
exercise	☐	☐	☐	☐	☐
play basketball	☐	☐	☐	☐	☐
play soccer	☐	☐	☐	☐	☐

B Write about yourself using the information in the chart.

_____

_____

_____

_____

_____

5

Complete this conversation.
Write the correct prepositions in the correct places.

Susan: What time do you go jogging *in* the morning?   (around / in / on)

Jerry: I always go jogging 7:00.   (<u>at</u> / for / on)

How about you, Susan?

Susan: I usually go jogging noon.   (around / in / with)

I jog about an hour.   (at / <u>for</u> / until)

Jerry: And do you also play sports your free time?   (at / in / until)

Susan: No, I usually go out my classmates.   (around / for / <u>with</u>)

What about you?

Jerry: I go to the gym Mondays and Wednesdays.   (at / <u>on</u> / until)

And sometimes I go bicycling weekends.   (for / in / <u>on</u>)

Susan: Wow! You really like to stay in shape.

6

Complete the crossword puzzle.

Across

4 Pierre never _____ . He's a real couch potato.

6 How often do you _____ yoga?

7 I like to stay in _____ . I play sports every day.

8 Jeff does weight _____ every evening. He lifts weights of 40 kilos.

10 Diana goes _____ for three miles twice a week.

Down

1 Andrew always watches TV in his _____ time.

2 Kate has a regular _____ program.

3 I do _____ at the gym three times a week. The teacher plays great music!

5 Paul is on the _____ team at his high school.

7 Marie never goes _____ when the water is cold.

9 Amy _____ bicycling twice a month.

A Read these ads.

**Do you enjoy the outdoors? Do you need exercise?
Do you like walking and meeting people?**

Join the Hiking Club!
Call 555-1191.

We go on a different hike every weekend.
Sometimes we go on a two-day hike
and camp overnight!

Adult Education Program at Monroe High School

Mondays to Fridays 6:00-9:00 P.M.

APPLES

la belle pomme

belle pomme

For more information, call 555-6845.

Fall classes: photography; computers for business;
typing and word processing; Chinese cooking;
Spanish, Portuguese, and Arabic language classes

Come to the YWCA or YMCA! Look at our new activities!

Aerobics, racquetball, softball, yoga!
For anyone from 9 to 90! Singles, couples, and families welcome.
Friday night, teen disco! Saturday night, seniors night!
Phone us at 555-7439.

B Where can you do these activities? Check (✓) the answers.

	Hiking Club	Adult Education Program	YWCA / YMCA
play indoor sports	☐	☐	☐
do outdoor activities	☐	☐	☐
take evening classes	☐	☐	☐
go dancing	☐	☐	☐
learn to cook	☐	☐	☐
meet new people	☐	☐	☐

8 Choose the correct responses.

1. A: How often do you go swimming, Linda?

   B: *Once a week.*

   - I guess I'm OK.
   - Once a week.
   - About an hour.

2. A: How long do you spend in the pool?

   B: _____

   - About 45 minutes.
   - About average.
   - About three miles.

3. A: And how well do you swim?

   B: _____

   - I'm not very well.
   - I almost never do.
   - I'm about average.

4. A: How good are you at other sports?

   B: _____

   - Not very good, actually.
   - I sometimes play twice a week.
   - Pretty well, I guess.

9 Look at the answers. Write questions using how.

1. A: *How long do you spend exercising?*

   B: I don't spend any time at all. In fact, I don't exercise.

2. A: How often do you   go   for a walk?

   B: Almost every day. I really enjoy it.

3. A: How long do you spend jogging?

   B: I spend about an hour jogging.

4. A: How good are you   at soccer?

   B: I'm pretty good at it. I'm on the school team.

5. A: How well do you play basketball?

   B: Basketball? Pretty well, I guess. I like it a lot.

10 Rewrite these sentences. Find another way to say each sentence using the words given.

1. I don't watch TV very much.
   I hardly ever watch TV. (hardly ever)

2. Tom exercises twice a month.
   Tom doesn't exercise very often (not very often)

3. Philip tries to keep fit.
   Philip tries to stay in shape. (stay in shape) ~~keep fit~~

4. Jill often exercises at the gym.
   Jill often works out at the gym. (work out) ~~exercises~~

5. I go jogging with my wife all the time.
   I always go jogging with my wife (always)

6. How good are you at tennis?
   How well do you play Tennis? (play)

11 What do you think about sports? Answer these questions.

1. Do you like to exercise for a short time or a long time?

2. Do you prefer exercising in the morning or in the evening?

3. Which do you like better, walking or jogging?

4. Do you like to watch sports or play sports?

5. Which do you like better, team sports or individual sports?

6. How good are you at games like basketball or tennis?

7. What sport or game don't you like?

7 We had a great time!

1 Past tense

A Write the simple past of these regular verbs.

1. cook _cooked_   4. love _____   7. visit _____

2. enjoy _____   5. study _____   8. wash _____

3. invite _____   6. try _____   9. watch _____

B Write the simple form of these irregular simple past verbs.

1. _buy_ _____ bought   5. _____ slept

2. _____ gave   6. _____ spent

3. _____ met   7. _____ took

4. _____ saw   8. _____ went

C Use two of the verbs above and write sentences about the past.

Example: _We went to a rock concert last night._

1. _____

2. _____

2 Use the cues to answer these questions.

1. Where did you go this weekend?

   I went to a party.   (to a party)

2. Who did you meet at the party?

   I met someone very interesting at the party   (someone very interesting)

3. What time did you and Eva get home?

   we got home a little after 1:00   (a little after 1:00)

4. How did you and Bob like the art exhibition?

   we liked (the art exhibition) a lot   (a lot)
              _it_

5. What did you buy?

   I bought the new Madonna CD   (the new Madonna CD)

6. Where did Jeff and Joyce spend their vacation?

   they spent (their vacation) in the country   (in the country)
                  _it_

37

3 *What do you like to do alone? with other people? Complete the chart with activities from the list. Then add one more activity to each list.*

watch TV
read the newspaper
go shopping
do homework
exercise
have a picnic
go to a sports event
cook dinner
take a vacation
go to the movies

Activities I like to do alone	Activities I like to do with other people

4 *Complete the questions in this conversation.*

A: How _did you spend your weekend?_

B: I spent the weekend with Joe and Kathy.

A: What _did you do on saturday?_

B: Well, on Saturday, we went shopping.

A: And _did you see/do anything special_ in the evening?

B: No, nothing special.

A: Where _did you go_ on Sunday?

B: We went to the amusement park.

A: How _did you like it?_

B: We had a great time. In fact, we stayed there all day.

A: Really? What time _did you get home?_

B: We got home very late, around midnight.

Answer these questions with negative statements. Then add a positive statement using the information below.

☑ have a boring time	☐ finish our homework on Saturday	☐ go out with friends
☐ watch it on TV	☐ work all day until six o'clock	☐ take the bus

1. A: We had a great time at Carrie's party. Did you and Jane enjoy it?

   B: *No, we didn't. We had a boring time.*

2. A: I stayed home from work all day yesterday. Did you take the day off, too?

   B: _____

3. A: I worked all weekend on my research paper. Did you spend the weekend at home, too?

   B: _____

4. A: I studied all weekend. Did you and John have a lot of homework, too?

   B: _____

5. A: Carl drove me to work yesterday morning. Did you drive to work?

   B: _____

6. A: Kathy went to the baseball game last night. Did you and Bob go to the game?

   B: _____

6 **Read about Andy's week. Match the sentences that have a similar meaning.**

A	B
1. He was broke last week. __*f*__	a. He had people over.
2. He didn't work on Friday. _____	b. He had a good time.
3. He worked around the house. _____	c. He didn't do the laundry.
4. He didn't wash the clothes. _____	d. He took a day off.
5. He invited friends for dinner. _____	e. He did housework.
6. He had a lot of fun. _____	✓ f. He spent all his money.

7 *Did we take the same trip?*

A Do you ever take summer vacations? What kind of vacations do you like to take: relaxing? educational? exciting?

B Read these reports about Thailand.

a temple in Bangkok, Thailand

William's report

We went to Thailand for our summer vacation last year. It was our first trip to Asia. We loved it! We spent a week in Bangkok and did something different every day. We went to the floating market very early one morning. We didn't buy anything there – we just looked. Another day, we went to Wat Phra Keo, the famous Temple of the Emerald Buddha. It was really interesting. Then we saw two more temples nearby. We also went on a river trip somewhere outside Bangkok. The best thing about the trip was the food. The next time we have friends over for dinner, I'm going to cook Thai food.

Sue's report

Last summer, we spent our vacation in Thailand. We were very excited – it was our first trip there. We spent two days in Bangkok. Of course, we got a river taxi to the floating market. We bought some delicious fruit there. The next day we went to a very interesting temple called the Temple of the Emerald Buddha. We didn't have time to visit any other temples. However, we went to two historic cities – Ayuthaya and Sukhothai. Both have really interesting ruins. Everything was great. It's impossible to say what was the best thing about the trip.

C Who did these things on their trip? Check (✓) the answers.

	William	Sue
1. visited Thailand for the first time	☑	☑
2. stayed for two days in Bangkok	☐	☐
3. visited the floating market	☐	☐
4. bought fruit	☐	☐
5. saw some historic ruins	☐	☐
6. traveled on the river	☐	☐
7. loved the food the most	☐	☐
8. enjoyed everything	☐	☐

8 Complete this conversation with was, wasn't, were, or weren't.

A: How ___was___ your vacation in Peru, Julia?

B: It _____ great. I really enjoyed it.

A: How long _____ you there?

B: We _____ there for two weeks.

A: _____ you in Lima all the time?

B: No, we _____ . We _____ in the mountains
for a few days.

A: And how _____ the weather? _____ it good?

B: No, it _____ good at all. The city _____
very hot, and the mountains _____ really cold!

9 Choose the correct questions to complete this conversation.

Namibian meerkats

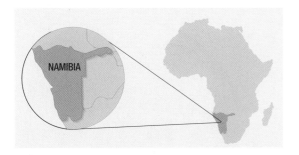

NAMIBIA

☐ And what was the best part?
☐ How long were you in South Africa?
☑ How was your vacation in Africa?
☐ And how long were you in Namibia?
☐ How was the weather?

A: _How was your vacation in Africa?_____

B: It was a great trip. I really enjoyed South Africa and Namibia.

A: _____

B: For ten days.

A: _____

B: I was in Namibia for about five days.

A: Wow, that's a long time! _____

B: It was hot and sunny the whole time.

A: _____

B: It was definitely the national parks and wildlife in Namibia. And we saw
some meerkats!

10 Choose the correct words or phrases.

1. I'm sorry I was late. I had to _____ a phone call. (do / make / go)

2. My friends and I really enjoyed your party. We all had a _____ time.
   (boring / good / funny)

3. I _____ some photocopies of the report and put them on your desk.
   (did / went / made)

4. We didn't see very much in the mountains. The weather was very _____.
   (cool / foggy / sunny)

5. I worked very hard in Switzerland last week. I was there _____ .
   (in my car / on business / on vacation)

11 My kind of vacation

A What do you like to do on vacation? Rank these
activities from 1 (you like it the most) to
6 (you like it the least).

___ go to the beach

___ look at historical buildings

___ go shopping

___ visit museums

___ spend time at home

___ have good food

B Answer these questions about vacations.

1. How often do you go on vacation?

   _____

2. How long do you spend on vacation?

   _____

3. Who do you usually go with?

   _____

4. Where do you usually go?

   _____

5. What do you usually do on vacation?

   _____

8 What's your neighborhood like?

1 Places

A Match the words in columns A and B. Write the names of the places.

A	B	
☑ barber	☑ agency	1. _barber shop_
☐ gas	☐ bar	2. _gas station._
☐ grocery	☑ café	3. _grocery store_
☐ Internet	☑ office	4. _internet café_
☐ karaoke	☐ phone	5. _Karaoke bar._
☐ movie	☑ shop	6. _movie theater._
☐ pay	☑ station	7. _pay phone._
☐ post	☐ store	8. _post office_
☐ travel	☐ theater	9. _travel agency_

B Write questions with "Is there a . . . ?" or "Are there any . . . ?" and the names of places from part A.

1. A: I need a haircut. _Is there a barbershop_ near here?

   B: Yes, there's one on Elm Street.

2. A: I want to send an e-mail. _Are there any internet cafés_ near here?

   B: No, there aren't, but there are some near the university.

3. A: I want to send this letter. _is there a post office_ around here?

   B: Yes, there's one next to the laundromat.

4. A: I need to make a phone call. _Are there any pay phones_ around here?

   B: Yes, there are some across from the library.

5. A: We need some gas. _Are there any gas stations_ on this street?

   B: No, there aren't, but there are a couple on Second Avenue.

6. A: We need to make a reservation for a trip. _is there a travel agency_

   near here?

   B: Yes, there's one near the Prince Hotel.

2 Look at these street maps of Avery and Bailey. There are ten differences between them. Find the other eight.

> **Grammar note:** There are; some *and* any
>
> **Positive statement**
> There **are some** pay phones near the bank.
>
> **Negative statement**
> There **aren't any** pay phones near the bank.

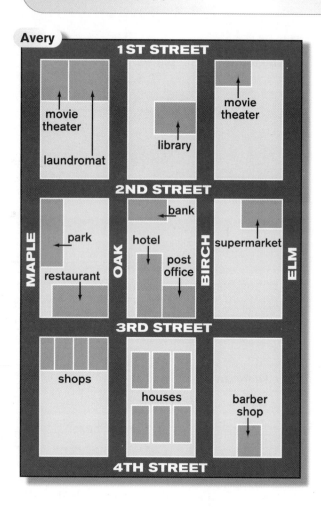

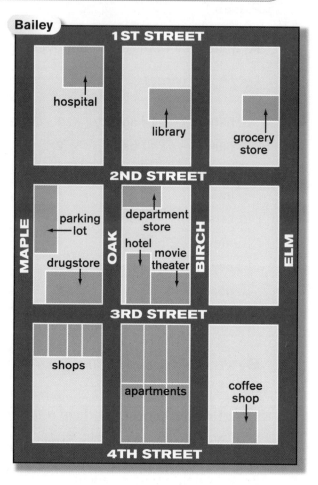

1. *There are some movie theaters on 1st Street in Avery, but there aren't any in Bailey.*

2. *There's a park on the corner of 2nd Street and Maple in Avery, but there isn't one in Bailey. There's a parking lot.*

3. _____

4. _____

5. _____

6. _____

7. _____

8. _____

9. _____

10. _____

3 Answer these questions. Use the map and the expressions in the box.

1. Where's the nearest bank?
   There's one next to the grocery store on 1st Avenue.

2. Is there a post office near here?
   Yes. There
   _____

3. I'm looking for a drugstore.
   _____
   _____

4. Is there a laundromat in this neighborhood?
   _____
   _____

5. Is there a department store on Lincoln Street?
   _____
   _____

6. Are there any pay phones around here?
   _____
   _____

KING STREET

grocery ← store

hotel

bank   movie theater

PALM STREET

1ST AVENUE

drugstore

2ND AVENUE

gas station

3RD AVENUE

library

A B C

LINCOLN STREET

laundromat

D

post office

YMCA →

RIVER STREET

| A | = | travel agency | C | = | gym |
| B | = | department store | D | = | pay phones |

4 Answer these questions about your city or neighborhood. Use the expressions in the box and your own information.

1. Are there any good restaurants around ~~school~~? *here.*
   yes there are, there are some good restaurants around here.

2. Is there a police station near ~~school~~? *here.*
   No, there isn't any police station near here

3. Are there any good music stores in your neighborhood?
   No, there aren't any good music stores in my neighborhood.

4. Is there a karaoke bar close to your home?
   No there isn't any karaoke bar close to my home.

5 *The grass is always greener . . .*

A Read these interviews.

Modern Life magazine asked two people about their neighborhoods.

Interview with Diana Towne

"My neighborhood is very convenient – it's near the shopping center and the bus station. It's also safe. But those are the only good things about living downtown. It's very noisy because the streets are always full of people! The traffic is terrible, and parking is a big problem! I can never park on my own street. I'd like to live in the suburbs."

Interview with Victor Bord

"My wife and I live in the suburbs, and it's just too quiet! There aren't many shops, and there are certainly no clubs or theaters. There are a lot of parks, good schools, and very little crime, but nothing ever really happens here. I would really love to live downtown."

B How do Diana and Victor feel about their neighborhoods? Complete the chart.

	Advantages	Disadvantages
Downtown	*near the shopping center*	
Suburbs		

C How do you feel about your neighborhood? Write about it.

_____

_____

_____

_____

6 Complete the chart. Use words from the list.

☑ bank   ☐ hospital   ☐ noise   ☐ people   ☐ school   ☐ traffic
☑ crime   ☐ library   ☐ parking   ☐ pollution   ☐ theater   ☐ water

Count nouns		Noncount nouns	
bank	_____	crime	_____
_____	_____	_____	_____
_____	_____	_____	_____

7 Write questions using "How much . . . ?" or "How many . . . ?" Then look at the picture and write answers to the questions. Use the expressions in the box.

☑ a lot   ☑ a couple   ☑ many   ☑ only a little   ☐ not any   ☑ a lot

1. (noise)   How much noise is there?   There's a lot.
2. (buses)   How many buses are there?   there aren't any
3. (traffic)   How much traffic is there?   there is only a little
4. (banks)   How many banks are there?   there are a couple
5. (people)   How many people are there?   there are a lot
6. (crime)   How much crime is there?   there is one criminal.

Choose the correct words or phrases to complete this conversation.

Luis: Are there ____any____ (any / one / none) nightclubs around here, Alex?

Alex: Sure. There are _____ (any / one / a lot).

There's a great club _____ (across from / between / on)

the National Bank, but it's expensive.

Luis: Well, are there _____ (any / none / one) others?

Alex: Yeah, there are _____ (a few / a little / one).

There's a nice _____ (any / one / some) near here.

It's called Sounds of Brazil.

Luis: That's perfect! Where is it exactly?

Alex: It's on Third Avenue, _____ (between / on / on the corner of)

the Royal Theater and May's Restaurant.

Luis: So let's go!

9 **Choose the correct words or phrases.**

1. I'm going to the stationery store to get some _____ .
   (birthday cards / coffee / food)

2. We're taking a long drive. We need to go to the _____ .
   (laundromat / gas station / travel agency)

3. I live on the 8th floor of my _____ .
   (apartment building / neighborhood / theater)

4. Our apartment is in the center of the city. We live _____ .
   (downtown / in the neighborhood / in the suburbs)